Books and Music by Indran Amirthanayagam

The Elephants of Reckoning, Hanging Loose Press, New York, 1993
Ceylon R.I.P., Institute for Ethnic Studies, Colombo, Sri Lanka 2001
El *infierno de los pájaros*, Editorial Resistencia, Mexico City, Mexico, 2001
El *hombre que recoge nidos*, Editorial Resistencia/Conarte, Monterrey, México, 2005
The Splintered Face (Tsunami Poems), Hanging Loose Press, New York 2008
Sol Camuflado, Lustra Editores, Lima, 2010
La pelota del pulpo (The Octopus' Ball), Editorial Apogeo, Lima, 2012
Sin adorno—lírica para tiempos neobarrocos, Univ. Autónoma de Nuevo León, México 2012
Uncivil War, Tsar—now Mawenzi House, Toronto, 2013
Aller-Retour Au Bord de la Mer, Legs Editions, Haiti. 2014
Ventana Azul, El Tapiz del Unicornio, México, 2016
Pwezi a Kat Men (written with Alex LaGuerre). Edition Delince,
Il n'est de solitude que l'île lointaine, Legs Editions, Haiti, 2017
Coconuts On Mars, Poetrywala, Paperwall Publishers, Mumbai, India, 2019
En busca de posada, Editorial Apogeo, Lima, Perú, 2019
Paolo 9, Manofalsa, Lima, Peru, 2019
Sur l'île nostalgique, L'Harmattan, Paris, France, 2020
The Migrant States, Hanging Loose Press, New York, 2020
Lírica a tiempo, Mesa Redonda, Lima, Peru,2020
Blue Window, Dialogos Books , New Orleans, 2021
Ten Thousand Steps Against The Tyrant, Broadstone Books, 2022
Origami: Selected Poems of Manuel Ulacia, Dialogos , New Orleans, 2023
Powet Nan Po A (Poet Of The Port), MadHat Press, 2023
Musica Subterranea, Editora Kotter, Brazil, 2024
The Runner's Almanac, Spuyten Duyvil, New York, 2024
Seer, Hanging Loose Press, New York, 2024
Let Nan Sid, Edisyon Fred, Gonaives, Haiti, 2024

Rankont Dout,
CD with Donaldzie Theodore, Pawol Tanbou, Titi Congo. Port Au Prince. October 2017

They Died Not in Vain,
music video, with Evans Okan, Cuernavaca, November 2019

The Runner's Almanac

Indran Amirthanayagam

SPUYTEN DUYVIL

New York City

Acknowledgments

Some of these poems appeared in earlier versions in Punch Magazine, Axion,
Live Encounters, The New Verse News, among other publications.

For Lola

Anandan

The Runner

The license to step

and write ten thousand

poems every day,

every night.

The author is doubly grateful to Lola Amirthanayagam
for the cover and author photos

CONTENTS

Note to Book

Do not go against the need
and desire to be one, to share

ribs and thought, to explode
all the received wisdom

and write the almanac
together as if for the first time.

The Runner's Almanac

The runner runs in my blood, in my mind
and heart; feeds from light and water,
wind and fire; recites recipes for food
I prepare, dreams I inhabit, books

I choose to bring to term. The runner
is a sign in the sky, a voice inside
the skin, a phrase in a poem. The runner
carries two x chromosomes to my x

and y but is not opposed, shares
the enterprise. I listen to her advice,
of when to plant, how to find balance
and leap ahead, how to create

perennials to assure the food supply
while experimenting with new lines.

RUNNER

You are running
out of the mountain,
across the bridge,

into the park,
running, wrapped
in a shawl,

protecting passing
walkers, birds, trees,
clearing muddied

thoughts, focusing
on ten thousand
steps, perfect

pitch. running
in my heart
beating in step.

my mind
composing
these lines.

THE MISSION

When a boy in Colombo I served
on the altar of the chapel next
to my grandmother's house.
My first day on the job I kneeled
towards the altar not realizing

I should have turned around
and looked instead at the parishioners.
The priest corrected me
and I took the lesson to heart.
Ever since I have looked out

at the world, to the public, to people
I mean to serve but with God
behind me, guiding me along.
Now, several decades later, I realize
I have become an older friar

in the monastery, privileged
to serve today's youth, my purpose
even clearer, to dedicate what
remains of breath, love and work
to spread the word of poetry.

LOVE AND ISLANDS

I love you, baby that's it. I ain't going back and I have passed Go and I don't
want any money but yes a meal with you from time to time a conversation
in the wee hours and in the middle of the day when desire becomes urgent,

and I would love to give you chocolates and flowers and tofu; propose trips
to the islands, realize them, to make summer in winter, spring in the fall,
and yes certain islands stand out from my particular journey so shall

we start exploring the blue green sea off Trincomalee, finger palms
on the Cornish coast, walk down the hill to Hanauma Bay? Shall we fly
as well over the Great Wall if that invitation crosses political barriers?

It would be a tough choice, holding off denouncing jailing of minorities,
thought crimes, lobotomies, until our return. Decisions, revisions...to what
extent should we engage, and how free is our speech? This poem began

and rests in love although it cannot avoid the temptation of social and political
melancholy. We cannot visit Eelam or have coffee with Ai Wei Wei in Beijing.

After Vallejo's Poem X

There is a myth, mythology, and many decades
of scholarship, thousands upon millions of readers
invested— saying *Trilce* is the mother church,

the original source of spring, the miracle of water—
remembering rain in Paris and a consumptive man
dying also of loneliness and heartbreak, but

the man's lines are not always sad, not always
black heralds. Look at this Poem Number 10,
birth foreshadowed in a sweet ten month love-in,

three mysterious, additional months absent,
then the nine month gestation, to come back
as a whale, the dove its sentry, announcing

the miraculous birth without violence,
the new mother sitting up in her hospital bed
to grease some nosegays, tranquil, content.

STRIDER

Keenness of feeling, desire to speak overwhelming
as I search for the right form to express overflowing
need to banish sleep, wake up running, dancing

to *Graceland, Aqualung, Lola, Yellow Submarine,*
and to you on the trail—sauntering in my sleep
then trilling in morning bird song, sporting rabbit

ears keen for the almost silent step of the photographer
before dashing off into the brush, fawning deer
surprised by the spring, drinking, woodpecker

even stopping its relentless eating just for a minute
as you run by, as you run this poem into a state
of atonement, of salvation, of bliss at the miracle

of life popping out from the dark, tangled interstices
of melancholy, where my heart had foundered,
until you whistled by, striding.

LOVE UNMASKED

I want to hold and calm you,
say this deep-gashed silence—

fish eye plucked out, leaving
a body throbbing blind—

will pass and let you harvest
morning light again, blood

stains washed away, letters held
in the drawer....I am comforted

they exist, that you can go back
through thousand sheets of

prose to find meaning, to share
love with strangers who become

friends visiting you on bookstore
shelves once we move again

into the physical world,
taking our masks off at the door.

Up to a Thousand Words

The picture emits hope,
faces beaming light
and grace, affirming
bonds shaped in verse,

in the interstices
between and within
lines, caesuras, dots.
The picture cannot

deny, speaks beyond
time, into souls
of lovers who
recognize

above the masks
the shimmering eyes.

Second Childhood

Mother needs care and I have played the role for five years and counting,
exhausting the good will of the audience (other family members, friends,
parishioners). It is time for my understudy to take over and for me
to sleep without dreams of failing to shave before the matinee,

of staying a bit too long in bed with my girlfriend, getting caught
in traffic, running to the staff entrance, doorman glowering, then
right on stage, lipstick on cheek, not in character, dutiful son not
ready to wrap his mother in swaddling clothes after her bath, bar

the bathroom door with his body scream when she tries to go back
to the shower where she fell asleep the other day causing panic
in the house. Thank God, I had not drunk or written too much
that early morning, and with help of rubbing alcohol and the kind

of heft adrenaline wakes up, I dragged her body out and across
the hall to bed. Is this the stuff of poetry? Written on the wall
of your screen? Will you contact the understudy? I am shy to admit
my limits, grappling with reality, reversal of roles, bloody tragic unity.

THE RUNNER SPEAKS

Sometimes I run a mile round
the neighborhood. Sometimes

I go for three, including a foray
on the trail. Sometimes

I storm out of the house to clear
my head of the thousand racing

thoughts. I have to study, yes,
do my day job even remotely,

cases piling up, and then poetry,
the rare fruit. Oh, to have time

to write. You are a lucky man
regarding time, inspiration.

but you have born your share
of hurt. You would have married

by now if plans had worked,
God always with another bend

in the curve I am running round—
for you to interpret—your verse.

LIFT- OFF

I don't want to sleep. Not
yet. Our last meeting
germinated a seed,

and wide-eyed I marvel
at the growing speed,
already a stem, bud

sprouting. Two days
later, in the post-
midnight hothouse,

I note the flowering
with a heart in my
farmer's almanac.

A THOUGHT, A TORTOISE

With you I am a tortoise:
patient, slow, like a late
summer lick of wind
tousling your hair.
I deliver your post on foot,
each step measured,
without haste, smiling.

Without you I count
starlings passing over
the field. Strip
the scarecrow and wait
for a new set of clothes.
Lay on the grave
a bunch of fresh roses.

Union of City and Country

You have joked about going local since the beginning
of confinement, local produce, local park to walk,
local girl. But chances of meeting the latter seem
bleak in the 'burbs for an expat New York City boy,
except when females come out with their dogs
and you time your stepping out, but then what
will you say to a spouse and her dog? Luck will

improve if you spot two women together with pets.
They could be sisters, friends. They may give you
the eye and you follow like a hound dog. You always
fancied yourself as Elvis but he became Costello and now
who will inherit Graceland but the state of Tennessee,
its Historical Society? Socialism, friends. On the West Coast,
nobody recalls the whisper of Hearst calling for his butler

but San Simeon stands like Ozymandias defying the arrogance
of individual man. The State of California is in charge now.
A comfort in the midst of today's generalized capitalist distress.
Some treasures will be conserved for the common good.
Washington D.C. lies just ten miles away as the crow flies,
this city boy within reach of the perfect union, of city and country,
Rock Creek Trail. My dear city sprite, let us meet along the path.

Before

I have been here before,
in silence, absence, sleep
robbing morning. I have
been here before, waking

up, taking stock, noting
elastic time, Sun still
lighting my window,
writing. I have risen

from the grave to consult
the angel on a gravestone
in the nearby cemetery
while geese pick worms

from grass, morning of
eating, man alive, walking.

MIDNIGHT RUNNER

The runner is my friend.
She lives in the city
and runs every day.

She runs in my mind
as well, along
the trail into

the country
where I stride
beside gravestones

on my morning
stroll in the cemetery
beyond the path.

One day I expect
to kiss the angel on
my favorite headstone

and march into
the woods instead
of going directly

home. That day
will shine like
midnight 1999.

GOD WALKING

You think God does not exist,
or if he does that he has gone
missing? I tell you.

you are wrong. I tell you
God is walking towards
me now. This morning

I saw him wearing white,
my son arriving at National
airport, my mother dressed

to the nines, in green
batik blouse, green pantsuit
walking out of the house

with a cane. No more
walker. Not today.
And my son said

she looked good.
She is on the mend.
Imagine that after

finding her, just
two weeks back,
slouched on a chair

hot water lashing her
from the shower.
And her helper thought

she had died. We used
smelling salts
and we dragged her

out of that sleep.
We are not sleeping
now. Soon we will

let the cane go flying.
Soon, we will say
to the woman running

out of the city along
Rock Creek Trail
and on the path

in front of our house.
Good afternoon.
Welcome home.

Perspective

Will you read, not between,
but the lines themselves?
The runner speaks. She is

human, not a gazelle,
a squirrel, a bird. The runner
observes the observer,

addresses the poet, sharing
thoughts and dilemmas
about her day-to-day,

noting that the poet
has time to be
inspired, to write.

BRIDGE

It's okay. *Tudo
bom. Pas de
problème.*

You have made
your peace, love
translated now,

gone to the other
side; and God
has not left

you behind,
given a new
reason to write,

running into
your life.

DESIGN

Impossible to know
God's plan, design,
why a friend of a friend
smiles broadly after

a reading, then becomes
an independent walking
companion in the city,
where from phone

to phone we speak,
"do you see the leaves,
yellow-green, wedges
on the sycamore trees?"

We met last summer—
a whole cycle
has gone by, while
the new world, born

after the virus,
ruptured the old
design, leaving
this slow

fermenting alliance
time to taste
right, this drink
a glad tiding.

On the Island

What shall we have for dinner?
I can go to market this morning,
pick up coriander leaves, parsley,

beans, potatoes, and aubergine
for us, and sardines for the cat,
then get back to peel and cut,

crush and blend whole spices
for the stew, put wild flowers
in a vase, dust the books

and find verses from Yeats
and Dickinson, even better
Hart Crane to recall

the last time we walked
on the Bridge, hands
clasped in Spring,

years between us
disappearing East,
vanishing

into the Atlantic,
by the Lady blessed.

To Go Ahead

One cannot deny what
grows with its own energy,
that feeds on interpretation
of facts in common, songs,
poems, letters shared since
we became friends in a reading,

what we love as much as food
or the dawn. No one knows
the future is truth we learn
but there is a counter argument,
from the person named by light,
that will not be extinguished

in a room alone, insisting
on entering the meeting
of all these elements,
the ceremony of accepting
the inevitable, the shared
life—going ahead.

Atomic Code

Not boy or girl-
friend, husband
or wife, not tied,
by contract
obliged, but free
atoms in love,
generous hearts
whirling on,
about, within
a point in
the petri dish
of the controlled
experiment,
dispersing time.

In Time

I am running on Oxford
Street, by the HMV. I am
running with Sparks and
Leo Sayer in my hands.

I am running with Tim Rice
in my ears, his Saturday
morning show, rock n roll
greats on Capitol radio.

I am running with Buddy
Holly, raving, raving.
running with Miss Molly,
up Blueberry Hill.

running to the bitch
on the bicycle who
called me nigger, sambo
gollywog when I first

got to London, to tell
her she will not hurt
me any more. I am
bigger, Notting Hill

in my brain, White Riot.
No more prisoner of
the ancient curse.
Burn and rebuild. Punk

Love. Without quarter.
Hate go take a walk.
I am the executioner
now and I am running

the cards with love.
Children, HMV was
a grand palace for
the long playing record

on Oxford Street.
And this song will
play wherever you wish
to remember or know

for the first time,
that we are running,
running with love,
not fear. In time.

Voice Mail, Music

Loved hearing your voice's
sweet register full of

light, robin flitting upon
frets and keys, strings

and piano lifting me up,
giving me leave to write

to you, to everybody, saying
thank you for checking in,

for my heart leaping.

Carnival Coming

I am telling you, carry the torch now: Kamau he gone, Derek before
him. But you are walking still on the Savannah and back to Belmont,
your belly flat, to spice the channa, stir cow heel into the soup. You

have always cooked your own food, writing perfect miniatures, stories
of little people in little houses with no back door, sea shaping island,
keeping lovers, hand in hand, on the beach. Now, the virus has entered

along with migrants and visitors. Everybody is afraid. Everybody
thinking where did this community hand-off begin. And you are there
saying stop sowing fear of the other, of the wide world beyond

the back door. Stop saying the Lord cometh Stop talking plague
and black death. But I am saying everybody so easily, and we without
a thought, blind to walls going up, fortress Europe, fortress Peru,

fortress United States. Politicians say these are temporary, to stop
SARS-Cov-2. But evil makes evil in its name, people blocked
from their dream, the promised land an illusion. What was

the world like I ask in 1999? What will our world become
after the vaccine, when planes start to fly and islands welcome
the necessary tourist dollars, and Benetton, world socialism

and the United Nations jostle to become fashionable
once more, and you walking the Savannah imagining
the next mask you will sew for the mother of all carnivals.

Testament

I have put away sad and jealous
feelings, exhaustion before
facing uncertain day, uncertain
night, competition for the prize,
hearts, minds. I have put all

this into poetry which you
can read when you have time...
Or your children can when
they come across my book
among your effects. And

the inscription. My story
is open but requires a decision
still to pull the book down
into the lap, to open the pages.
I am already speaking quaintly,

the screen our page, and therefore
I am too a page, displaying
post after post in hopes
that you will stop and
read, ping back.

God And His Children

You did not break my heart,
God played his part so I might
learn that my heart is like life

on earth, a turtle born on the beach
who enters the sea for the first time.
Will he survive? He enjoys all

your gifts, Lord, strong organs,
lungs, a shell. But I ask every
father and mother if they would

let their children go to school alone
on the first day, the school of life
where the heart may break but will

find the force even so, divine wings,
to return to the beach and celebrate
life lived, the blessing of living still.

In The Green Room

One day goes by, alright, a second
in slow ennui, getting harder,

by the third I need to cry your name,
see you comb your long hair,

tease a coquette's smile. I am stuck
on you my dear, love every minute

we can share and the dream of
your growing to receive accolades

we give the best in our tribe.

INSUBSTANTIAL

Even if our bodies are taken,
our minds are free to love
each other until time ends
this history, writing on
the screen, on the urn,

on stone. Then I will
become what is called
delicately in literature
a zombie, visiting every
night for our party.

From an Elder

I understand the delicate
nature of your task, your role
as the eldest of the family,

but please remember
your siblings have grown up,
most of our children as well,

that we must respect
the basic right of every
person to a private world,

to negotiate with codes
learned from experience,
that we are no longer

keepers of anyone except
of their basic rights, to be
left alone, to trust their paths,

to let them walk on their own.

SAD BLUES

Feeling sad, turning
to song. feeling
blues not with you

feeling blue but
don't have to let
this feeling through

except on keys,
page, screen,
in what you read.

Need to lift this
sadness; place it
somewhere...

where...here but
no worries, healthy
the right way

to overcome, the only
way to go on friend.
So I go on writing

remembering when
I used to sit down
in a cafe, at dinner,

with you. Now I eat
at my desk laptop
that's alright, sadness

turning to song,
blues disappearing
into screen.

BLUE

In the bracing cold I walked,
looked through trees and saw
the bay's waters silver blue;

a blue jay flew by as if
on cue and I pivoted
my camera in a flash

as the white bobbing tail
of the deer exploded into
the blue morning; and I

kept repeating the mantra
of the true blue anorak
I sported my first day

at primary school, a color
chosen by the chestnut-
haired Pauline for her own

coat. She slipped a locket
in my pocket on that last day
before we went off to separate

grammar schools and the rest
of our lives. I thought
she had mistaken her pocket

for mine. I realize now
that love cannot always
speak, the stone inside blue.

LOVE IN THE NEW WORLD

A lover's duties contain
the contradiction during
the farewell, that you must
let go to keep memory intact,

allow winds to blow back,
to accept the scent of temple
flowers again, a return
to the starting block

in birthplace, or new-found,
New World island
twin, renewed, ready
to embrace the woman

running along the road,
without a care, who
catches the scent,
turns and stares.

GOODBYE SWEET COCONUT

Goodbye Sweet Coconut. lick
of water, scoop of flesh, cutting,
husking at the roadside stand

on the way north, mid-morning
thirst satisfied, sun-blessed skin
in the far away isle, brilliant

waking, memory's vitamin
coursing in the blood. I love
you 'though I cannot touch

or eat you. I love you but
I will go on with my day-
to day, Sweet Coconut,

seeking new water, new sun,
recognizing once and for
all that I cannot replace

you my sweet sap, up
and down the tree, into
the pot, toddy. And on this

East Coast of the United States
near the Chesapeake Bay
I say out loud words I need

to let you go. To let you go.

Light Words

Your words are light.
When you speak
I feel alright

like a seed
entering earth,
sprouting groves

of tomato,
avocado, onion.
When you ping

me out of sleep
I become dizzy
before turning

into a rare
earth-sealed rod.
I can do everything,

dance on much more
than a pin. Put sleep
away for the day

and march into
woods, not feel
a wink at all, ready

to soar like the geese
who are taking off
in front of my eyes.

THE RUB

I miss you, not by choice. Once
opened the heart cannot close,
except in Emergency a team

of doctors sewing it up after
blocks have been removed.
My remote monitor, *My Air*

device is advising via email
that I have had a few more
events, interruptions, this last

week *Are you getting too much
or too little air?* Perhaps you
should have a clinical review?

It does not understand love
and its energy bursts, intense
rubbing of the meteorite

fragment discovered
on Rock Creek Trail
burning to bone, the bone.

THE GIVE AWAY

We have to be serious now. Mother has begun to eat
the daisies, and we need to keep her in check. She is
the same person but more extreme, her generosity

without bounds, craftiness as well. She gets on
the phone and asks for a ride to church knowing
she has gone already in the morning, calling

this friend and that one, to catch a mass at the next
parish, or even in Washington at the cathedral.
One Sunday, during a heavy rainstorm, she left

the house with one of her enablers, front door
unlocked. She cannot manage a key, fingers
arthritic, able barely to grip the cane she places

next to her chair like a flag. Carry that flag, Mother,
and walk like the royal you are, but do not think
you can outsmart your humble servant, your child.

I too pretend to the crown. I will not go to the grave
a dauphin, an also-ran, a minor character. Bring out
the fine wine, rare scents, hidden olive oils. Bring out

the Madrasi sarees. Bring out of your mind the elephants
bedecked with sapphires we treasured in London
before you gave them away, Mother, in a fire sale.

HAND EXERCISE

I have forged my path,
made my bed, and read
a large number of the great.

But my fingers are numb,
blood not flowing to tips,
yet I type. I must keep

the small bones limber,
write over sadness and fear.
She will go tomorrow

to lead her new life
and I will turn to the wood,
to my daily walk. Angel,

stay with me. God, help
blood flow well into
my last redoubt, this

instrument of hands,
to spill all the blear
thoughts out.

Truth in Eleven

What say you about
the fleeting passage,
whether you reach
maturity for seven
years or seventy, what
will remain in the mind?
Did you bring light?
Heal a broken heart?
Walk across the bridge
when nobody cared,
cars whistling by?

FAREWELL, MORNING

Time has slowed to blinding, cloying instants,
gazing at a distance your body tousled in sleep
speaks to me of powerful moments when time
stopped in the past, waking up in Morne Calvaire
on Sunday morning then dressing to walk uphill
to the Nonce's house, plumerias giving sweetness
to the early morning walkers in fine raiments off
to meet the pastor and praise God. Go in peace. Go
with God. We had his blessing then. We have it now.

LOVE FLITTING ABOUT

At day's end the smile matters on the lips
of one who has realized a dream, who has
made someone else happy, who has given

to one in need, That particular smile
has no price, cannot be commodified.
It comes from the heart and its spiritual

root, that what one gives, gives back.
So out of this pandemic I rise with three
new books in hand. Out of this loss of

a partner I rise knowing she is smiling.
at peace with her choice. I too am smiling
through tears knowing I cannot imprison

love, and love comes back in another
song, from a bird at hand I did not think
would sing for me but has appeared

now, a bit sick, in need, at my window.

UNDRESSED

Lie with me
tonight.

Wrap me
in skin,

shimmering
skein,

to wade
together,

into
that pool

deep
in woods,

to bathe,
melt,

disappear

A Triple Baptism

You have to face the beloved and declare
your love and say you will never ever
see her again. That happened to me
once in an airport parking lot after
a few days of a lovely visit. It happens
across the planet, in homes and gardens,

walking around the neighborhood:
the alchemy of love and the alchemy
of falling out of love, the mystery
of the thrilled pulse and the faint
heartbeat puttering out. So why make
another love poem? Why contribute

to the ten thousand kilos of literature
on this dart-induced and death-defying
subject? The organ in the body will beat
and send blood to the top of the head
and the tip of your toes. That heart beats
when in love or bereft. It belongs

to a genetic calling card. You are
on earth for an allotted time whether
Cupid pricks or lets you wander
by in a monotonous haze. But those
who believe in nurture, lovers
of experience, say that one learns

to measure that beat, to shape it
according to circumstance, to be able
to live alone. I say such experiments
will not result in any panacea, vaccine
or escape from the lines written
in your hand, that say you will have

three children and the last will come
late, a surprise. How can this be I ask
my hand as I turn into another decade
and have no mating prospect? Ah,
the hand never lies. The child comes
dressed as an idea for the annunciation,

the glorious revelation. The lines
are a rune. Here's the rub. You
have made three books, three
children this Covid season.

LOVE YOUR NEIGHBOR

God gave you a son and daughter,
father and mother, brothers,
a sister. Your parents brought
you up. Now it is your turn
to care for mother in her old
age. And so it shall be when
you too will need your son

and daughter to come and do
the needful, to care for you
when ill and feeble. You are
lucky to have children. What
about those whose kids
have been taken away, shot
in the street, in a foreign land

fighting for some vague motive
in the head of a headless
government? What about those
who have nobody, who must
depend on the village, on a friend?
Let us remember the neighbor.
Let us take care of each other.

An Irish Sojourn

I dreamed of you this morning. A delicious stay in bed.
Slow-moving from kiss to rhythmic dance, to shouting
with a keen sense of glee. I am, if not elegant, at least

a strong suitor although I recall I allowed a few blue
shrieks to sally forth while straddling the back
of your filly and galloping off beyond all the Irish hills

to the Galway coast where we laid our ponies to rest
and dipped into the salty-fished, bracken-rid sea and rose
and bobbed like a mermaid and a *merboy* over the crests.

DIARY ENTRY

Have you considered
a woman of your age,
experience and station,

mature, divorcee, seeker
of discreet solutions
to biological need,

willing to experiment,
good friend
with a large bed

in the heart, someone
with whom you have
grown up in the career,

who does not represent
a goddamned theft
of innocence and beauty?

The Open Secret

The blear cloak is wrapping me up
this evening but I will ignore it. I have
work to do, dreams to fashion. I wish

to share them with you in this poem,
my public invitation to go out, to kiss,
to snuggle. Will you reply?

Mask Man, One Island

Taylor, *tailleur*, *taliare*, cutter,
with scissors, needle, thread,
seamer, working cloth to fit
dimensions of the man, sway
of the woman. Taylor,

sequined, dotting the mask
with semi-precious stones.
Taylor, poet reading
Brooklyn jazz. Friend,
confidant, thank you

for the hand-sewn, unique,
indelible clothes, visions
through the back door,
landing at the Port and
greeting old schoolmates,

together in the *country*
of warm snow, writing
from island to island,
Trinidad between Hudson
and East Rivers, Labor Day

Carnival bringing all roosters
to roost, Belmont, Savannah,
Flatbush, spun in the same roll
of cloth, every Shrove Tuesday,
every Labor Day, masked.

No Woman (Trenchtown Blues)

I am learning to live alone again
in the romantic sense, to eat sardines
from a tin and bread and yogurt

from *Trader Joe's*. I cut garlic,
ginger and onion but don't make
curries. No one to eat them

in confinement but me. My mother
lives in the middle room but can
only take soup, Campbell's

or some Italian variety. I have
poems to write; must make
my bed still, gather clothes

for the washing machine,
the day-to-day reviewed,
the shared duties contract turned

into one for a sole proprietor,
individual tax payer, but head
of household still (My mother).

I depend on the car, the store
and money, a job. I still have
the latter, typed at a distance

from the city. I am lucky. There
is no better time for this refresher
training in living alone. I will return

to the stage blissfully experienced
and leaner given that I don't make
rice or pasta, and eventually. or sooner,

I will die, if not from old-fashioned
botulism or our new world plague
but from a broken heart, dare I say it,

that did not heal fast enough. Do excuse
the bathos. I don't fancy bathing this
morning, rubbing my back with the back

of my hand, a contortionist, ideal example
of the nuclear individual, with money
and poems, but no woman, crying.

River Walk

I walk by the river every morning. After rain
the water turns muddy and churns, forming
a small rapids over the stony bed. I wonder

about depth, whether I would sink
or swim. And what to do with my I-phone
in case I decide to jump? The Japanese

man fishing on the side, would he give up
his bait and dive in after me as I float away?
Too much to ask. Let him fish in peace…

and let me get on with my dying
in a less public way. Back at the house.
In the room of my mind.

The Dream

I write verses to express myself. I can cry out loud walking in the woods.
or buy canvas and make a crude painting in primary colors. I can sing,
dance before the mirror listening to the radio from Rio. So thank you God

for these options. The persona in Cardenal's "Epigramas" wrote that
because of unrequited love he went out and threatened the government.
I have renewed my purpose, writing and translating. I have railed against

the government as well, on the birth island, during the denouement
of the Civil War when many thousands of civilians were butchered,
along with the usual victims, soldiers, rebels. I have never given up

hope. I understand I have resilience, a stoic center that will not
be flustered although the lachrymal glands are working overtime
and demons ride horses in my literary nightmares. And there lies

a way out of this mess. Turn all experience into a story, a tall
or short tale spoken into the laptop, published in a magazine,
a book, Some would say stop dissembling. No more fiction. I reply:

go fly a rat. Don't bother me with your insistence on historical truth.
There is something more vital to survive the loss, and even start
to flourish. Make the metaphor. Make it new. Make the old new.

Fall in love again even in the mind. Seek happiness. Don't whinny
any more in the paddock, snort in the sty. Break out baby. Write.
Find. Join the Ra rah. Rejoin the Labor Party. Go for a longer

walk every morning along the Rock Creek Trail until one day
you arrive in the city ten miles away and a runner passes by
dropping her bandanna and you pick it up and say, is this yours?

Morning Rescue

Key residents of my heart have found
new loves, are smiling and hopping
along pavements in their hometowns.

Some are driving for the first time.
Others are planning the making
of babies. All are sharing food

and kisses, wine and voyages.
As for me I am writing, hoping
that those who have not yet

coupled will glance at these words
and give me a call, as you just did,
Muse turned into voice, dear friend

who decided to greet me, giving
birth to this morning song.

To God and A Lady In the Shadows

Ay, God, you have got me twirling,
reeling in the challenge of your hook,

the levels of hurt, first the rupture
of the relation, then the new life

apart while I draw on the inexhaustible
well of emotion and shared histories

to write love poems that must stop
now to keep myself sane and redirect

the emotion to some new, old friend
who may just become the partner

You took away with brute force, pulling
out the canker of my older confidence

at the beginning of this pandemic.
To teach me a lesson about pride?

Or to bring me back where I belong,
walking along the shore at Jacmel Bay

dreaming of a free America and
Manuela Saenz? But I am moving

away into myth and history, and
my need is also prosaic, real. Call me.

LIGHT CONSTITUTION

A blast of light on the tree after
the storm gone north, woodpecker
pecking, robin rising on the breeze

between two branches, a man
stepping out on his constitutional,
setting organs in order, surveying

the woods for plants blasted by
last night's wind—not many branches
down, the passage swift, and the woods

come out standing, and now the party
of light showering trees, morning birds
flitting about, a man—striding.

Word Print

Prepare sweetmeats and fragrances, pick
flowers from your garden and make a garland,
then fill the basket you will carry to the temple
to feed your god. She gives you phrases,

word music and she too needs to eat,
to be strong. You are married to her,
don't forget, although you had no formal
coupling, no signing of an agreement before

a judge or priest. You married the first time
you found relief for your heart on the blank page,
then filled the page again and again as words
flowed in tears becoming ink—a man

drying on a mountain slope, conserved
near a temple—a scroll, a print.

THE FLAME PASSING

I realize now that writing will keep me occupied, away
from the source of my sadness, but like a vaccine that lasts
for only a season, even distilling in verses cannot give me
life-time immunity. No, I must face solitude without
a pen or any other crutch. I have to face it with my full

mind and heart and not give in to temptations—to walk
this way, a few feet, to the edge of the precipice, look
at the shining palaces below, then walk some more—
and falling realize the vanity of human vanity,
the illusion that I could have had marriage, wealth,

tranquility and a rich well of poetry, and loving
children, and a morning walk counseled by an angel
I met in the cemetery near the woods, who left her
stone dress on the plinth and flew into my mind,
to say keep your eyes focused on the deer in the bush,

the cardinal's flash as it flies by, and listen to your heart
beating and let it beat not only to pump your blood
through the country of your bones, but to be made
into words and song in the mind and its vocal chords—
these lines I compose to remember that the struggle

and the road always appear long, tough and blinding
in the smoke of loss, the sad turning back to see
one's home blasted in a flash, the forest fire that arrived
without warning on the hill beyond the backyard,
disguised as a virus, as bad things happening,

NEAR THE RIVER

Let the reggae play, slow and sway, we are not
by the river but we are okay, we will find
friendship in need and bring her water, serve
her wine, outside, even in Rockville, the town

center, a tavern open to evening light, clinking
glasses, unfurling grape leaves, and we will let
the reggae play in our minds, slow and sway,
we are not by the river but we are okay, under

the sky, undressing leaves, glasses sparkling,
saying you can sing of politics and bringing
scoundrels to the river to baptize and make
them God's children. But for now, let

the reggae play, slow and sway. We can 't
transform the city in a day. We can't save
all the people all the time, but we can
sit down under the evening sky stripping

grape leaves, clinking two glasses of iced wine.

SEEKING LIGHT

I am sleeping with dreams and nightmares.
They visit from the day-to-day, from
decades ago, the first time I walked

in a graveyard and defied death by making
love. My friend has disappeared from
daily prayers but remains a spirit roaming

at night, unbuttoning desire. I invoke
her now to say that no one will be forgotten
in my daily walk in the nearby cemetery.

I will name everyone who has held
my hands, embraced me, said go ahead,
you are on the right path. I will pray for you

now as I pray for clarity in the haze, a light
towards which I can walk, clapping my hands.

Tying the Strands

Love is not practical. It surges from unexpected, buried
depths of experience. It tempts with the forbidden, stepping
over unmarked yet firm lines. Do I, you, we, dare? Throw

convention out. Build a life together for a good twenty
five years before I must leave the stage according
to statistics, but perhaps by then we would have raised

a child with great love, who would become a brother
or sister to the children I have already, and a grandchild
to your parents and my mother, and beyond to our relatives

in the ancestral land. And we would dance a fiery jig
in Western dress at the prenuptial party, and then
on the day, march in a grand procession, shift

our eyes and hands in bharatanatyam, praise
and thank God in veshti, turban and gossamer saree.

LISTEN...

I want it straight, guide me if you can (or if alone
I will search online) what fridge to buy to replace
the oversized one turning warm, and where

to place it. Then what to do with the two thousand
pounds of books. And where shall I put the old
hand-carved furniture. Shall I give up the storage

space? Bring the stuff back to the house for
one last look before shipping it out to the street?
Rid the house of memories encrusted in wood,

paintings, papers? When I do this I will move
light as a bird riding an air current, effortless,
turning myself over and over again, a baby

tossing in mother wind's arms, smiling.

Sempre (Always)

Our private lives would have entered
the field of the page from time to time,
a photograph, a slant of light, a stroll

on a boardwalk, by the river Thames,
recalled in verse. But the images
would have come unwilled, appeared

when time decided, not you or I,
because time was not measured
then; it had not ended. Now

that we are apart, time has coiled
back, a writhing snake, its head
snapped, but embrace of life

and desperation not slunk away,
not dead in peace. Hence, this
tsunami of remembrance, this

place of memory, these verses
I write for you inexhaustible
like the sea or the wind where

they will ride in a bottle,
wrapped in the feet of a pigeon.
No matter what happens in daily

life, the foods you eat, ointments
you rub on your skin, friends
you keep, these verses will fly

on the wind, in the rumor
of waves, and peep through
curtains in the window

of morning, a stream
of light. I hope to make
them until time ends.

A Hint of Spice

I love you so I cannot stop
my mind from writing

invitations, to come with me
to the mountains, to stroll

on a bridge over
a stream and watch geese

cleaning feathers on shore
before wading in, honking

to the sky while we smile
overlooking the water,

noses snuggling, cheeks
and nostrils flaring

at the mildest hint of
some far-away Indian spice.

GALWAY WOMAN

I know a woman in Galway
now. Kinnel has gone
to the shade, and Brian Friel
from Omagh as well. But cows,

sheep and peat smell still,
and sea air from beyond
the hill, and the taste
of milk and butter, poems

spread on morning bread,
and looking out of
the picture window
into fields where you run

and run towards me
speaking my name.

Free Sonnet, Spilling Over

Facing the rest of my life, alone again, yet not alone,
son and daughter, mother, friends, poems. Yet alone
in bed, in the study, at your empty desk, the closet
filled still with your clothes. Maybe this will pass

or I will keep the room as parents who have lost
a child keep her room as it was, washing sheets
every week, putting flowers in the vase. But
in my head I am not alone. It is full of commotion,

elephants charging, the large, wet rat of my nightmares,
beautiful birds, sunsets, women, and lots of ideas
jostling about to be translated into poems. So why
write this lament? Why complain? Why make

the poem a constant site of warring dilemmas?
Write outside of the head instead. Write from

history. Dig into ecology. Imagine thoughts
of a Neanderthal tricked by Homo Sapiens.
Think of Helen doomed, the rape, swan
escaping, howling with laughter. Think

of justice for all, justice in bed, on the desk.
Justice or peace. A stopping of charging
in the brain, what nirvana means,
enlightenment, shanti. It is finished.

SEEDING

I have farmed fields across the globe,
planting avocado, tomato, chillies, and love
in diverse regions. The avocados thrived,

the root and leafy vegetables, love plants
as well, although many suffered blows
from wind and movements abroad. But roots

remain fresh, and I have learned
that I only need to prune dead leaves,
give the plants a good watering

and they will be renewed and I will feel
loved again, in multiple celebrations,
across languages and physical borders. Love

is in the air, in digits now, and though it may
not give a back rub or body slam, it counts,
friends. The kiss you send through

the internet I feel on lips and tongue. I kiss
you back. I kiss your neighbor for good
measure. I invite you now in this post-midnight

hour to a planetary love-in. Just post the word
Seed on your walls. Do it for me who has
plenty to share, and with all of you.

The Scented Dream

A sad business, our lives apart, this cloying summer afternoon
when scents that caught us on the vine are blossoms bursting
into fully-exploded flowers, as birds flit about mating. Incredible

how life thrives beyond the window, and some of it wants
to come inside, inchworms, caterpillars, spiders, but larger
creatures—squirrels, birds and cats—usually respect borders,

realizing they live in a parallel world to their observer's,
who lives now, like them, passing by at night when you light
your lamp in the window, scampering out of the day's bush

when the dream of our reunion—coming together
for a feast after interminable days in wilderness—flashes
like a daydream beside an oasis in my mind.

GETTING OFF

I will dance my life, please don't
worry. I will bop my shoulders,
rock my head. twaddle and waddle,
shake and bake, step out and stutter-

step, fox trot, boogie woogie. I will
even if my heart is reported shot,
head exploded, memories falling
like shrapnel, and I must find

another heart and spirit
to pick up the casings,
to clean up the mind's house,
while life keeps dancing

on the carousel, musical
hearts turning round, round.

SIGNAL KEEPER

I wait for your call. I go for
a walk. I photograph the sky.
I return to our bedroom, then
turn to the zoom reading,

wander off to the kitchen,
prepare a slight dinner,
stare again at the screen,
think about whom else

I can call, then start
to leaf through my contacts.
Reading literature and watching
a film are distant memories,

I need to talk now and write.
You are my first correspondent,
proverbial other half. You have
the option of first refusal,

but send me a signal, so
if necessary I can keep going.

Love, More Fitting

I don't believe I am dreaming
in darkness. We agreed to keep
our minds open, so I am filling

that common ground with images
from the book we began to write,
that got caught in the hurricane

but is bobbing still in waters rising
almost to the roof, that will decline
while we are rescued or climb

down on our own, and life returns
to a rhythm it recognizes from
the past, but which is renewed

with learning shocked upon us
from these days in the wilderness.

Revelation

I am another and the same,
and I am looking still for
the relationship that lasts,
and while looking discover

that I already have one
I did not realize until now.
So I will stay, no matter
what happens, open always

to your call and that
of our director, the little
creator. I have waited
a long time I say

to my notebook,
to play a principal part
in the drama of life
and I am not going

to lose the chance.
I have the stage directions,
my beard is shaved.
To the American union

I raise my hand, my glass.

Love in a Box

It is good to make up a box and start to put endearing objects
inside, your winter boots, snazzy spring shoes, and then,
but I am not there yet, contents of the chest of drawers,
scarves, pants, a couple of sarees, blouse, bands we kept

for the quiet ceremony at the courthouse. Eventually I will
get to photographs, the album, the framed ones, and also
hundreds stored in the Cloud, Or I won't. I will just let
them be. Rome was not conquered in a day nor love

managed in a box. But the box is a good idea, a book
as well where I write our love's events, trips, evening walks
under the light of the setting sun. We can all relate, dreaming
as we read of the get-away. Now the get-away will be boxed,

and the box covered by a shroud, until you come to take it
away—not of course photographs or images in the Cloud
of the head. Those items cannot be boxed, or erased, or swept
away. But I agree, my dear, it is a good idea getting a box.

DIVINE INTERCESSION

I will face this roaring current
just in front, a step forward
but I will not stumble, I am

confident in the power of spirit,
of mind to say beyond here
I will not tread. The malicious

spirit who guided me to this
crossing and said, run,
scamper, slide into the water,

then whorl, plummet over
the falls—I will not give
him the last word. I will

not be swept away. God
has stopped me. God
has told me to turn.

PRODIGAL

The flame burns in Paumanok, streaks the White
Mountains, flashes across the Adirondacks, splashes
in Cold Spring, wherever you wish to light, the candle

is infectious and the world catches fire, banishes
pandemic, replaces Covid with something older,
grander, love, my child, baby face, love in a blade

of grass, love in the stag coupling with the doe,
in these words typed directly into the heart of
absence, without absinthe, with hope and bubbling

joy, with insane optimism, that tomorrow like
today the prodigal children will come back home.
They are here now and I am soaring over mountains,

hurtling through the sea, a human bomb
exploding into ten thousand rose petals of shrapnel.

Not Out

"Wickets are falling fast, and Basil is bowling off breaks"
— *Mervyn Taylor*

Wickets are falling fast,
my friend, but you are holding
up your end smacking every
loose ball to the fence. Basil

may be bowling off breaks
but you read his line, his turn
tucked away down the leg side
for runs every time; your stand

unveiling my front garden
again when Tom Graveney
came to dine with Basil
d'Oliveira, Imagine those

stars in 1966 eating string
hoppers with the family
at Kynsey Road, and Basil
bowling to my brother

and I before the great banyan.
That was boy-dreamed eternal
life, before we retired the next day
to the match at the Colombo Oval:

England versus Ceylon. Now
England is poetry, a record shop,
primary school, off to Lord's
on a Saturday to see Lloyd,

Kanhai and Kallicharran
smack bowlers everywhere,
and so much more, the line
heavy, dense, packed, bursting,

and Ceylon a tuck shop,
a civil war, tsunami. How
many lines, verses, books?—
and cricket despite everything,

always blood, always
sorrow, always perseverance,
batsman not out, innings
declared, match drawn.

THE STRIDER TESTIFIES

I used to write from the bottomless hole, abject
sorrow, black on black. Not any more. I have
found peace on the riverbank, in the living room,
walking in the neighborhood forest. I don't cry.

I smile, laugh, dance with the male bird chasing
the female through the thicket. I sit on the bench
and smile at joggers in their tracksuits swirling
past my spectacles, the spectacle of hair swaying

and pert form staying pert, and I don't mind
recognizing that I am stirred with the stirring,
life racing past everywhere I go and me
observing, walking, sitting. But who is

looking at me? Who notices that I no longer
brush my hair, that I stride careless, carefree?

THE GUEST

Mother is furious, unleashing
everywhere, the storm no
longer giving reason to curl
up with a book but to run,
although there is nowhere
to hide, to run to a gym,
a reception hall, but
the tornado turns
to the door, insists
that it too has an invite.

Post Silence

I took a vow of silence a few days ago
but failed to let you know. I make amends
now. Silence has fed me well. I have

looked at myself and not taken a photograph.
I have called an old friend or two with whom
I had dropped out of touch. I should explain.

My vow concerns poetry, written utterance.
Silence in metaphors, rhyme and meter.
But not speech. I remain part of the human

family of languages and I am delighted
to share what I know in voice notes,
video recordings, and in real-time chats.

I remain committed to exchange
but ephemeral aspects of it, gestures
that accompany words, penetrating

looks at the telephone screen, but just
to be doubly clear, no selfies. I have
gone beyond that phase, entered

a new world with new rules, post-
pandemic in the midst of the pandemic,
a future adjustment in the present,

and I am forever young as the song
said once, in the moment missing
you terribly but willing to persist

listening to the sounds of...oh dear,
I think I am suffering from
the condition where one repeats

old tunes like a broken long-
playing record. Enough. Love U.
Enough. *Até mais.* See you later.

THE PATH

We turn to the Greeks when we don't
understand the events of our lives, why
relationships end, for example, the role
of fates and furies, miscreant gods.

We turn to Christ in need, asking
for guidance, help through the vale,
and a miracle. We approach our mother
and other powerful spirits for prayers.

And if, at hand, we drink a glass
of scotch because that is a traditional
medicine burning through sadness,
cauterizing the wound. But soon enough

the headache wakes up, and we go for
a walk in the woods, and write one poem
after another, speak to friends, and find
ourselves alive, that we have survived.

Lines about Bread

We turn to the Greeks when we don't understand the events of our lives,
why relationships end, for example, why you will never again serve me bread.

TELL THE LIGHT

Tell me to turn my eyes,
to look away, to shift
my heart. Tell me
we can only express

feelings in poems.
Tell me to focus
energies on ambition,
on bread, on Haiti,

Africa, everywhere
but this bed filled
with sixty-year young,
old expiring, reviving

flesh, writing to you,
morning light rising.

GUIDE

The runner runs in my blood, sees
the road and trees and passing birds

through my eyes. The runner beats
a drum pulsing in my veins, feeds

me intravenously. The runner speaks
without speaking, cries in silence,

laughs in cascades of flooding
waters, and I am swimming,

rolling and nothing will stop
me from reaching the ocean

of being, to swim for a last
time across to the country

without a hat. But
the runner is pulling me

back. Not yet she says.
Write. Keep running.

INDRAN AMIRTHANAYAGAM is a poet, editor, publisher, translator, youtube host and diplomat. For thirty years he worked for his adoptive country, the United States, on diplomatic assignments in Africa, Asia, Europe and North and South America. Amirthanayagam produced a "world record" in 2020 publishing three poetry collections written in three different languages. He writes in English, Spanish, French, Portuguese and Haitian Creole. He has published twenty four poetry books, including *Isleño (R.I.L. Editores)*, *Blue Window (Ventana Azul) (trans. Jennifer Rathbun) (Diálogos Books)*, *Ten Thousand Steps Against the Tyrant (BroadstoneBooks.com)*, *The Migrant States*, *Coconuts on Mars*, *The Elephants of Reckoning* (winner 1994 Paterson Poetry Prize), *Uncivil War* and *The Splintered Face: Tsunami Poems*. In music, he recorded *Rankont Dout*. He edits the Beltway Poetry Quarterly (www.beltwaypoetry.com); writes https://indranamirthanayagam.blogspot.com; writes a weekly poem for *Haiti en Marche* and *El Acento*; has received fellowships from the Foundation for the Contemporary Arts, the New York Foundation for the Arts, The US/Mexico Fund for Culture and the Macdowell Colony. He is the IFLAC Word Poeta Mundial 2022.

Amirthanayagam hosts *The Poetry Channel* https://youtube.com/user/indranam. New books include *Powèt nan po la (Poet of the Port) MadHat Press, 2023)* and *Origami:Selected Poems of Manuel Ulacia (Diálogos Books, 2023)*.. Indran publishes poetry books with Sara Cahill Marron at *Beltway Editions* (www.beltwayeditions.com). *Let nan sid* is forthcoming from Edisyon Freda in Haiti. Amirthanayagam's first collection in Portuguese *Música subterranea* has been published in 2024 by Editorial Kotter in Brazil. *Seer* is forthcoming in 2024 from Hanging Loose Press.

www.ingramcontent.com/pod-product-compliance
Lightning Source LLC
Chambersburg PA
CBHW020919140626
46545CB00015B/929